Kersal Moor

Sweet falls the blackbird's evening song
In Kersal's poised dell;
But the skylark's trill makes the dewdrops thrill
In the bonny heather;
Wild and free
Wild and free
Where the moorland breezes blow.

Off have I roved you c
Where tinkling moo
Sing all day long, their l
To the lonely listen
And croon at n:
In pale moonli;
While mountain breezes blow.

GW00568444

So wrote Edwin Waugh, the Salford dialect singer, 'Lancashire's Burns,' in the 18th century.[1]

Much has changed the Moor since that time, although it still retains an atmosphere of mystery, undisturbed nature and peace, quite detached from the frenzy of 21st century life.

It was not always so. This small piece of moorland has witnessed some amazing episodes of social and political history, from public executions to the biggest political rallies of the 19th century.

For those of you who do not know Kersal Moor and its rich social and political history do read on, make a visit, stroll its pathways and reflect on its natural beauty and its dramatic and significant influence on so many lives.

What's in a name?

The name Kersal, Caersael or Keres-al was first recorded in the twelfth century and has Saxon derivations. Its mixture of translations include: 'a wood of elder in a boggy place' and 'a heath in the bend of a river.' All this suits Kersal, which has also been referred to as Kersal Moor and Kersall Wood. Kersall with a double 'l' was the spelling used on the map of 1848 but not on the map of 1895. It was the Hamlet of Kersall when it was presented to the Cluniac monks in 1142; it was still a hamlet, in the township of Broughton, when it was amalgamated with Salford in 1853. The residents objected to this because they did not wish to be 'assimilated with the cotton of Manchester or the filth of Salford.' The advantage they were going to get, however, was an upgraded drainage and sewage system.[2]

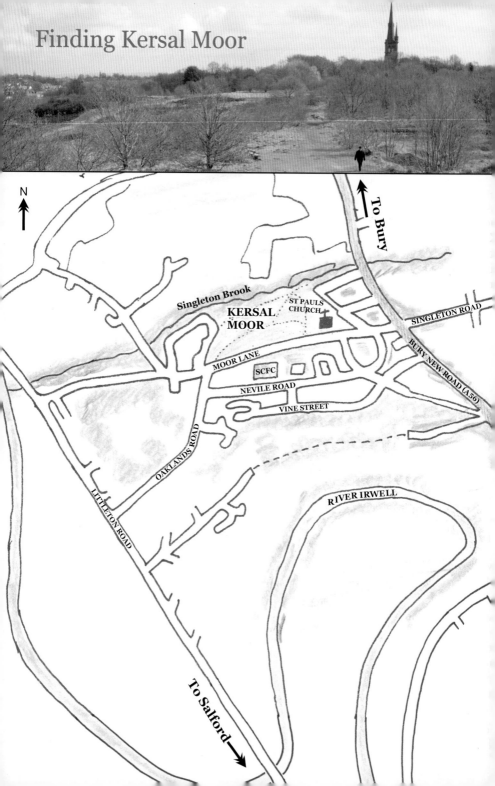

Finding Kersal Moor

N

To Bury

Singleton Brook

KERSAL MOOR

ST PAULS CHURCH

SINGLETON ROAD

MOOR LANE

SCFC

NEVILE ROAD

VINE STREET

BURY NEW ROAD (A56)

OAKLANDS ROAD

LITTLETON ROAD

RIVER IRWELL

To Salford

SO HOW DO YOU GET THERE?

If you travel along the Bury New Road [A56] just fifteen minutes and two and a half miles from the centre of Manchester and turn left, at the little white Toll House into Moor Lane, you will find Kersal Moor. Look for St Paul's Church, with its unique twin spires, over 160 feet high and there, hidden behind a thick boundary of trees, lies Kersal Moor. Stop and take a path into its centre. Here you should pause, look, listen and imagine, for this Moor has many tales to tell.

The Moor in bloom - cheery trees

As you move along the pathways you will see much blossom, whether it's spring or summer. In the spring there are yellow catkins, soft grey pussy willow and the pink and white blossom of cherry trees and the one apple tree.

In the summer, the dog rose tangles with the brambles and the gorse is heavy with its bright yellow pods, which in the autumn turn to silver velvet. The heather is the delight of the Moor, as it gradually opens its tiny pink flowers, turning to deep purple in late summer.

There are rare plants such as the acid and wavy hair grasses and, towards the Singleton Brook, huge swathes of

Sweet smelling gorse in bloom

Himalayan Balsam, an invader of great virility and beauty. One wonders if this exotic plant was brought over by the wealthy upper class families of Broughton and Kersal, who indulged in the Victorian passion for collecting foreign plants and insects. Rev. John Clowes, who owned much of the Moor in the 19th century, was nationally known for his collection of orchids and had special glass houses built for them. Some of these were even named after him.[3]

Invader - Himalayan Balsam

It is its rarity of plants that led to the Moor being designated a Site of Biological Importance [SBI] in 1993 by Greater Manchester and listed for conservation by Salford City Council. The main focus is on the acid grassland and lowland heath, which are the UK's

Kersal Moor today, autumn 2008

Kersal Moor 19th century painting from postcard, artist unknown

rotected biodiversity habitats.

[See p.38 for biodiversity list]

The 'Plant a Tree for 73' Project was taken up with vigour by the children at the St Paul's Primary School, then on the Moor. Now there is a rich variety of trees from laburnum, cherry and apple to native trees, such as horse chestnut, sycamore, holly and great canopies of oak.

If you walk the Moor in the autumn, you will notice a thick carpet of acorns. Oak saplings are now spreading across the heather and there is talk of a tree management drive to thin them out.

If we could step back to Victorian times we would find a less woody and more spacious Moor. Look at the two pictures opposite - one from the 19th century and the other from today. The pictures not only reflect the radical change in the vegetation of the Moor but also the changes in its use.

LET US TAKE A WALK INTO THE HISTORY OF THE MOOR

We can explore as far back as geology can take us. The Moor is composed of course gravel and sand. This is known as a 'fluvioglacial ridge,'

Sandy paths on Kersal Moor

many of which formed along the River Irwell valley during the melting of the glaciers at the end of the ice age. The sand is in evidence all over the Moor. After heavy rain the sand is exposed in 'run off' even as far as the houses in Nevile Road, which runs parallel to the Moor, and once was part of it.

In the last century it was an accepted activity for local builders to source their sand and gravel from the Moor. This digging changed its contours because records show much higher gradients. People say that the hills of Wales and the Pennines could be seen on a clear day from Sandy Hill, the highest point on the Moor.

PEOPLE OF THE MOOR

The Neolithic Families

Archaeological digs inform us that the earliest settlers were Neolithic families, attracted by the supply of chert and flint, from the River Irwell basin. This they would shape into knives and scrapers, some of which can be seen in the Manchester and Salford museums. Charles Roeder carried out his own digs on the high point of the Moor from 1886 and found many examples of such tools. Today, locals still find artefacts, but usually they are clay pipes from Victorian and Edwardian times.[5]

The Romans

Historians have recorded the movement of the Romans through Manchester [then Mancunium] and on to the north. What is Bury New Road now was one of two Roman roads going north out of Manchester, one leading to Bury and the other to Lancaster. These two roads were joined by what are now Moor Lane and Singleton Road, leading to a ford of the Irwell at Agecroft. Roman pottery, found in the 1980's at a dig in neighbouring Rainsough, proved that this high spot was used as a Roman 'look-out' camp. The plentiful game and fishing would certainly make the Moor an attractive spot to camp.[6]

The Cluniac Monks

Later activities on the Moor had a religious flavour. Way back as far as 1142, an order of Benedictine monks had rights to the Moor, granted to them by King Stephen. Here they would fish, pasture their animals and keep bees for honey and candle making. The River Irwell was then 'rich with trout, grayling, perch, carp, bream and eels.' [This was not the case in the later 19th century when the Industrial Revolution turned the river to mud and all fish life died!]

The Kersal Cell, dedicated to the hermit St Leonard, originates from this time and its Tudor replacement can still be seen down by the banks of the River. This has its own fascinating story.

Royal Patronage and the Aristocracy

The dissolution of the monasterie by Henry VIII, in 1539, bought all thi religious patronage to an end. Nine o the Kersal monks were executed fo treason and from then the land wa granted to various aristocratic familie This was the way the King guarantee their loyalty to him.

The Hamlet of Kersal move between different wealthy families ove the next two centuries and include James Chetham of Crumpsall an Edward Byrom, whose son, Dr Joh Byrom, became the famous 18t century poet. It was the marriage o Mary Chetham to Samuel Clowes i 1772 that transferred ownership o much of Kersal to the Clowes family. I 1775 another section of Kersal wa purchased by the Clowes family extending the estate to include the lan north of the Irwell up to Vine Street.

The Story of the Mr Cribb and the Manchester Moth.

This is an interesting and sad little story from 1829. In June of that year Robert Cribb, an amateur entomologist from Manchester, was wondering the Moor. He came across some unusually moths, bright orange in colour with five brown spots on their wings. They seemed to have their habitat in damp and decaying alder trees close to the Singleton Brook. Mr Cribb collected many of these moths and generously gave a female specimen to his friend, another collector, named Wood.

Mr Wood passed the specimen on to a Mr.Curtis, who, at that time, was compiling and numbering a record of British Entomology. He recorded this new moth in the seventh volume on pl. 304 and gave it the name 'pancalia woodiella' in honour of Mr Wood. As you can imagine poor Mr Cribb was quite upset at not being acknowledged as the finder of the moth, since this would have made his name in entomological history. He refused to let anyone else have, or even see, any of his specimens.

His story gets worse! In order to get a loan, he left his moth collection, as security, with his landlady. Sadly, when he went to retrieve it, the landlady, fed up with waiting, had burnt the lot! The moth turned out to be the last of its species and apart from three examples; one being in the Manchester Museum, the moth is believed to be extinct. Other insects and moths, believed to be extinct, have turned up again, so keep your eyes open when down by the brook![4]

The Moor and the Civil War

The Moor played a part during the Civil War of 1642-49. There are many references in Salford to Oliver Cromwell, with roads and pubs being called after him. This seems to indicate his presence in the area. There was even a statue of Oliver Cromwell in front of Manchester Cathedral looking towards Salford almost in defiance.

Manchester was a Protestant city and Salford supported the King. Certainly Cromwell's Roundheads were billeted on the Moor, ready for any attack.

John Byron, the wealthy landowner, who lived at the Kersal Cell and was a secret Jacobite, is said to have travelled through an underground tunnel from the Cell to the Cathedral for Jacobite meetings. Likewise the Bishop could travel by tunnel from his house, then in Singleton Road, to the Cathedral.[7]

Research by the 'Salford Star,' however, throws doubt on the claims of Cromwell's presence in the area.[8]

DAYS AT THE RACES

Before the end of that century the Moor had taken on a very different character. From 1687 the Moor was chosen as the perfect venue, with its good gradients and sandy light soil, to be the Manchester Race Course. It was stated to be, ' one of the finest circular horse courses in Great Britain,'[9,10]

If you walk the Moor, along the most prominent and well-worn path, you are walking on what was once part of the racecourse.

The first official race was advertised in the London Gazette on May 2nd 1687.

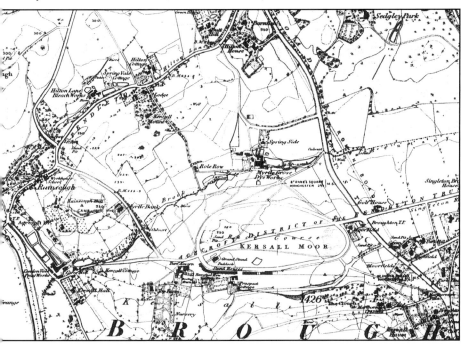

Map of Broughton showing Kersal Moor racecourse, 1847

'On Carsell Moor, near Manchester, on the 18th a race run. The Horse marks to be given in four days at the Kings Arms in Manchester.'

To get into a London paper showed it was of national interest. The races drew in crowds, from all classes, and radically changed the atmosphere of the Moor.

Each race included three heats of 4 miles each. Many races were for two competitors challenging each other. The track crossed Moor Lane and along what is now Nevile Road, to the finishing post at the current Salford City Football Club grandstand. In fact some of the cobbles of the racecourse still exist under the grand stand.

The races were quite lucrative with 'plates' awarded each day of £20 and

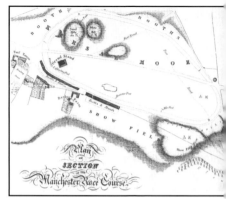

The Manchester Racecourse

£40, and even climbed as high as 10 guineas; an immense amount of mone in those days. Then, of course, there wa betting, which appealed to those wit little money but lots of hope!

The races also attracted th

A day at the races - sketch of the Manchester racecourse on Kersal Moor taken from last race programme in 1847

harpsters' and pickpockets. Records f petty crimes on race days tell of niscreants' caught 'selling obscene rints, picking pockets and gambling ith paper and dice.' Deputy Constable braham Driver of Broughton also ecords the case, in 1834, of James illington charged of gang robbery of iree men on the Moor. The punish-ient was 'to be transported beyond the eas for the term of his natural life.' That ieant Australia.

For many however, it was a gala day ut, away from the dirt and smoke of the ills of Manchester, especially at the /hitsun meetings, when there was a eal festival atmosphere. Quirky fun vents occurred, included male nude ices, said to be an opportunity for males to, 'study form' before choosing mate!! Not quite 'Ascot' although a lot f subtle parading and display goes on Ascot today!

Oliver Heywood, a non-conformist inister, wrote in his diary, ' there was a range, unheard of race on Kersey Ioor, near Manchester, in which, antily clad women took part!' High iks indeed!

Cock fighting, popular for betting, ok place every morning and there was n assembly each evening during race eetings. There is little reference to the iture of the assembly but may have en a planning meeting or simply cial followed by a trip to the Turf avern.

The races became so established at in 1777 a fee-paying Grand Stand as erected near the fenced horse iddock. In 1778 a Ladies Grand Stand as added, which sold tea and cakes for adies and gentlemen,' every ednesday and Friday and was even a nue for ladies flower-arranging

meetings. The grandstand stood in front of the Turf Tavern, which would be opposite the corner of the current Oaklands Road. This Tavern was owned by the Clowes family, as was part of the racecourse. One can imagine that it did great business on the race days, with vast quantities of ale being drunk.

Even Dick Turpin was reputed to be a regular at the races and in the Tavern. 'No person was given permission to sell ale or any other liquor, in any hut or place on Carselle Moor but such as are contributors to the races.' If they set up any other stall there was a charge of 1/- and those with lotteries paid 6d each. As can be seen it was quite a financial venture benefiting the owners of the Tavern. However, the Census of 1841 recorded the 'sellers of ale' on the Moor.

These 'entrepreneurs' probably operated in between the race days and lived in the 'booths' used on the Race Days. The Census, which was taken on the night of 6th June, recorded many people living on the Moor in these 'booths' and other temporary buildings. They may also have worked as dyers and salters at local mills.

The racing was seen by some as decadent and Kersal Moor as a scene of 'drunken debauchery!' Influential churchgoers, such as John Byrom of the Kersal Cell, forbad the clergy from attending the races and even forced the closure of the race meetings for 15 years. In 1846, on the death of Rev.John Clowes, his heir Colonel Clowes, decided not to renew the lease and the races were then moved to a new site at Castle Irwell, in the bend of the River Irwell.

The last meeting on the Moor was quite eventful with the partial collapse of the grandstand, injuring many and also a jockey fell and later died. Not a happy ending to what was such a glamorous period in the history of the Moor, lasting for nearly 200 years.

A current resident of Nevile Road, who lives just yards from what was the finishing post for the races, romanticises, ' I think of those horses pounding down where my house now stands and I can imagine the thrill, smell the dust and almost hear the cheers!' The noise of the crowds, with their raucous touting, their rowdy and excited cheering and the stamping of the horses, does seem a fantasy when one stands on the Moor today.[10]

Other Sports on the Moor

Between the race meetings archery was practised on the Moor, including longbow archery. In the eighteenth and early nineteenth century, the archers of Broughton, Cheetham and Prestwick were nationally famous and a club called the 'Broughton Archers' met at the Turf Tavern. In fact, Rev. John Clowes built a dining room on to the Tavern for the Archers to meet.

Golf was another 'gentlemen's sport' that featured on the Moor. Wealthy businessmen set up the Manchester Golf Course in 1818. It was a tough course of 8 holes, and with its sandy hollows and hillocks, was difficult to play. The area was used also by the public so was a little dangerous for those having a stroll! It was the second golf club to be established in England and was quite exclusive. The Club continued to play till 1862 and still exists today as the Old Manchester Golf Club. Although it has no course of its own it plays as a visitor at other courses. Golf was later played on the land south of Vine Street which had an impressive Golf Club House.

Another golf course can be see today from the Moor, rising over th hills towards Prestwick and across t Rainsough. This is Prestwick Gol Course and may have had some earl connection with the original Kersa Moor golfing fraternity.

The Moor and the Military

During this period the Moor was use also for large military reviews. Variou regiments held spectacular parades o marching, mock fighting and even hel their annual inspections on the Moo Records include the Rochdale Stockport and Bolton Volunteers i 1796 and 3,000 members of th Wiltshire, Buckingham, Louth an Stirling Militia in 1812. Charles Roede mentions finding spent rifle bulle during his 'digs,' maybe from suc events.

Not quite so jolly!

A rather macabre event was th public execution in 1787 of Joh McNamara. His crime was the theft c three waistcoats, two silk handkerchie and £8 in cash from the Cheetham house. He was charged as being one of gang that had terrorised the area fo some time. At 10 am on Saturday 11t September a procession left the Ne Bailey prison in Salford and, wit church bells tolling, proceeded on two-hour slow parade to Kersal Moo McNamara sat in an open cart for all t see. As it happened McNamara, a Irishman, had been charged fo political offences in Ireland and was t be transported. However, he escaped t England and, without an income, too up a criminal life. The execution scen on Kersal Moor was one never see before and drew immense crowds. Th gibbet was erected on an elevated spo clear for all to see and 'take note.' It wa eft there for some days to reinforce the message. But it was rumoured that it ailed to achieve its aim as a deterrent, ince pickpockets still 'worked' below he gallows!

An interesting poem, written at the ime, shows an enlightened view of the pointlessness of the death penalty.

The Execution of McNamara.

It was in the year that McNamara was hung,

When the heart that was feeling, by feeling was wrung,

For the wretch whom the law had with justice decreed

Had made forfeit of life with wicked misdeed,

Was from Lancaster dragg'd, for the idle as show,

By mistaken policy, adding to woe

Severity, such as a sentence ne'er said;

Nor tortur'd before death-but hanged until dead, dead.

To the wicked, example this had no gain,

And the sight of the wretch to the virtuous gave pain.

Joseph Ashton. 1790.

THE CHARTISTS COME TO THE MOOR

We move on and come to perhaps he most important event in the history f the Moor, one that aimed to change he political life of the nation.

Few people today would know that his little piece of land was a place of political significance. This could be heir lack of historical knowledge or ecause we often take for granted the fforts of others to achieve what we so arelessly under-value.

Kersal Moor was the scene of some of these efforts, with two enormous rallies held by the Chartist Movement in the 1830s. These demonstrated the feeling of injustice that existed between the social classes at the beginning of the nineteenth century.

To understand this hostility we need to look briefly at the social and economic conditions of the time.

A look at 19th century society.

At the beginning of the nineteenth century only the aristocracy had the right to vote. The middle class was amassing great fortunes from the textile revolution and gaining increasing economic power. However, these wealthy mill owners, like their workers, did not have voting rights. In fact, Manchester did not have an MP, whereas some rural areas with very small populations did.

The new gentry of bankers, merchants and industrialists, together with the aristocracy, owned 70 percent of the land of Britain and felt they had a right to a say in Government policy. Landowners such as the Chethams and Clowes family owned much of the Kersal and Broughton area and employed many people, who were often tied tenants. This restricted the freedom of these workers, because they were dependent on the landowner for both 'bread and board.'

A painting, by William Wyld, entitled 'Manchester from Kersal' and listed as 'Manchester from Higher Broughton' was commissioned by Queen Victoria in 1852. It is in the Royal Collection. It shows an idyllic pastoral scene from the Moor down to the River Irwell, with a background of smoking chimneys in Manchester and Salford. Another painting done by Rev.John

Waddington in 1856, entitled 'a View of Manchester from Kersal', showing the same pastoral scene, is in the Manchester Art Gallery. Here many grand houses were built by the new moneyed classes. This life style, with its clean and unpolluted environment, was in stark contrast to that of the working class, who lived in poor unsanitary hovels, working long hours for low pay.

These appalling conditions were described by Fredrick Engels, a German immigrant, who worked at his father's textile factory in Weaste and spent much of his spare time visiting the poo parts of Salford. He was a radical autho who recorded the abject misery of th working class in these areas. In hi book, 'The Condition of the Workin Class in England.' he described stree after street of poorly constructed, back to-back houses, sometimes shared b more than one family.

This was the focus of his discussion with Karl Marx, which led to their co authoring of the 'Communis Manifesto' in 1848. Their economi theories, expounded in 'Das Kapital' ar

The Influence of Peterloo Massacre, 1819.

In 1819 the Peterloo Massacre occurred on St Peter's Field, which is now St Peter's Square, in the very heart of Manchester. A meeting was called as part of a campaign for the reform of Parliament. What was a peaceful gathering of 60,000 people, turned into a bloody massacre in which 19 people were killed and over 500 were injured. One third of the demonstrators were women, all dressed in white as a sign that the protest was to be peaceful. The Manchester Magistrates panicked and called out the Salford and Manchester Yeoman Cavalry, special constables and even a 6-pounder gun. The cavalry were reported as 'wildly using their sabres', as the crowds tried to protect their Speakers: Henry Hunt, Richard Carlile and others.

Most of these people were angry at the mechanisation of the weaving trade and the growth of factories, which left domestic workers, who used handlooms, without work. In fact, in 1812, 30,000 troops from Wiltshire, Buckingham, Louth and Sterling regiments had been camped on the Moor ready to deal with any trouble from these Luddites.*

James Wroe wrote his 2 penny pamphlets, printed by the Manchester Observer, describing the Massacre. These became part of the influential propaganda that bolstered the anger of the people in the next half century of campaigning.

*People who objected to mechanisation of the weaving trade, named after Ned Ludd, [12]

ften referred to as 'the books that hanged the world.' They spent time together in the Chethams Library just near the Victoria Bridge, which was the boundary between Salford and Manchester. [11]

The end of the Napoleonic Wars, in 1815, had increased the number of unemployed and a mass immigration of Irish, as many as 34,000 to Manchester, swelled this number. The Irish were fleeing from the 'potato famine,' which resulted in the death of thousands of working class Irish. Many of these Irish were also dispossessed of their homes and shipped on subsidised passage to either America or England.

Between 1801 and 1851 the population of Manchester grew tenfold. This contributed to the bitterness and caused conflict between the unemployed from both countries.

Those working in the mines also felt the distress. Coal was needed to generate power and the miners worked up to 14 hours in dangerous conditions for little pay.

In 1818 coal miners, from Pendleton, demonstrated on the Moor and put their case for an increase in pay from 14 shillings to £1 per week, for a 12 hour day. The workers in the mines often included women and children. This was not made illegal until the Coal Mines Regulation Act of 1842, although a 'blind eye' was often turned on these employees and it continue for some time after this date.

The 1832 Reform Act, which only granted voting rights to the middle class, was a great disappointment for the working class and left them with little hope. They called it the 'Great Betrayal.'

The aristocracy saw the working class as uneducated and, therefore, unable to make decisions on matters of state whilst the middle class worried, that if the workers got power, their profits would suffer. Hostility between the owners of production and their labourers continued to grow, leading to a rapid strengthening of Trade Unions, often working with the Friendly Societies.

A new newspaper, the Manchester Guardian, reflected this tension in its reporting and, in 1821, led a campaign for economic reforms.

In 1838 Richard Cobden founded the Anti-Corn Law League, based in Manchester. This was a campaign against protectionist laws that forbade the import of foreign cereals and kept bread artificially high.

The situation was desperate for all labourers. By 1838 over 50,000 workers in Manchester and Salford were either on short time or unemployed. [13]

So the scene was set for the biggest Chartist rallies of the 19th century.

Back to the Chartists.

The Chartist Movement, driven by fervour for economic change and universal suffrage, was an amalgamation of the demands of Trade Unions, the Ten Hour [working day] agitation and the Anti-Corn Law League. It supported a six point [People's] Charter that it believed would change the lot of the working class and establish a fair and just political and economic system. Drawn up in 1836 by the London Working Men's Association, it was taken round the country and presented at mass meetings in major towns, particularly in the North where there was greater hardship and bitterness.

The People's Charter demanded:

- Universal male suffrage;
- Annual Parliaments;
- Vote by ballet.
- Abolition of the property qualification for MPs.
- Payment of MPs.
- Equal electoral constituencies.

This Charter was written as a Bill to be presented to Parliament by some radical Members of Parliament and, in true democratic style, was to be explained and accepted by the people.

On Monday, September 24th. 1838, the Manchester Political Union and the Manchester Suffrage Association sponsored a rally on Kersal Moor. Its purpose was to vote on the Charter and elect delegates for the Chartist National Convention. The Speakers included John Fielden, J.R. Stephens and the Irishman Feargus O'Conner, noted throughout the country for their firey oratory and powerful leadership.

O'Connor announced, 'So help me God, I am determined to have universal suffrage, or I will die in the attempt.' These were almost the same words spoken by Nelson Mandela in South Africa, more than a century later, when fighting the same cause. Whereas Mandela was sentenced to life imprisonment, O'Connor went to prison for 18 months from April 1845 till August 1848.

The Chartist 'Hymn'

Sons of Poverty Assemble

Rouse them from their silken slumbers,

Trouble them amidst their pride,

Swell your rank, augment your numbers,

Spread your Charter far and wide,

Truth is with us,

God himself is on our side.

Imagine this stirring anthem, bein sung by thousands of people on Kersa Moor. A sense of righteous emotio dominated the day.

The size and strength of this rall was beyond anyone's expectation and i difficult to imagine on today's tranqu Moor.

It is recorded as being the bigges political event of the 19th century wit estimates from 30,000 (Th Manchester Guardian) to 300,00 (The Morning Advertiser) Whateve the true figure, it was certainly impres sive.

Prior to the rally large placard covered walls for 10 miles aroun announcing the event and requestin mill owners to close for the day, so tha workers could attend. The mill owner fearful of losing income from poo attendance, reluctantly closed.

Special pleas to women to atten went out, 'on whose exertion depend the success of this glorious enterprise Many were involved for weeks in th making of the colourful banners tha decorated the march, proclaimin demands for justice and libert Although little mention is made of th role women played, it was an essenti one. Most working class women, an even their children, worked in the mil and coped with the hardships of dail survival. Apart from general poo health, cholera, typhoid and TB wer common diseases and the burden c these usually fell upon the wome There were many branches of Fema

A NEW SONG ON THE GREAT DEMONSTRATION

WHICH IS TO BE MADE ON KERSAL MOOR, SEPTEMBER 24TH 1838

by J. Wheeler

You reformers of England and Ireland attend,
To this song I have made which has lately been penn'd
Concerning a meeting which now has took pace,
Our rights for to gain and to better our case
The time it is come boys, the work has begun
To be free, or forever be slaves.

You Lancashire lads, this day is the time
Reformers will now both their hands and hearts join,
For Freedom and Liberty's now is the cry,
To no longer be slaves but like Freemen to die
So let us be steady, determined and ready,
When met boys upon Kersal Moor.

The rich man he lives in his luxury at ease,
The poor ma's degraded, death stares him i'th face,
The rich knows not now what to eat, drink or wear,
The poor's clothed in rags, what does the rich care,
But our motto shall be 'huzza for liberty,'
Now we're met boys upon Kersal Moor.

From Macclesfield, Stockport and Oldham they've come,
Ashton, Rochdale and Middleton with music and drums,
Bury, Bolton and Leith, it is a grand show,
Reformers all marching, Thou stands in a row,
With banners to free and loud shouts of 'huzzas'
Now Reformers join on Kersal Moor.

The Manchester lads now they lead on in front,
As they did in the days of the brave Henry Hunt,
Annual Parliament, Suffrage, determined to gain,
The Ballot, without these we slaves must remain
Determined to be either bondsmen, or free,
United on Kersal Moor.

The Birmingham lads and the lads of the North,
Have showed us great courage their valour and worth,
Will the brave men of Lancashire now behind lag,
All that do their heads ought to be stuck in a bag.
But no's all the cry, we fight till we die,
For liberty on Kersal Moor.

There is Fielden, brave Allwood and Oastler so free
Fletcher, Stephens, O'Connor, who all do agree,
Reform it is needful, Reform we will have,
For Freedom's the cry of the honest and brave,
Be loyal and brave boys, think on Peterloo,
Remember this is Kersal Moor.

You Fema'es of England all join the true cause,
Your liberty's rights, brave freedom and laws.
That in after ages our children may say,
Our forefathers struggled, fought for liberty,
And joined the throng now we bravely move on,
To the meeting held on Kersal Moor.

So up and be doing-in one Union join,
That the bright star of freedom may brightly shine,
And liberty's shout resound from shore to shore,
That Britons are free and will be slaves no more,
Huzza for Reform, we shall weather the storm
At this meeting upon Kersal Moor.

Chartists, one being in Hume and another in Chorlton. These Manchester female Chartists sent out a message to their, 'Sisters of England, Ireland, Scotland and Wales,' saying, ' if ever there was a time when it was our duty to shake off our apathy and engage in a grand struggle for liberty, surely it is now...' The raised fifty pounds, a lot of money at that time, to have a special banner made, depicting O'Connor for the Kersal Moor Rally. They did no shout 'votes for women,' seeing thei demands for better pay and condition as the same as for men, The time for thi would come and that is another grea story.

Let us try to imagine a gathering c so many people.

Over seventeen trade contingent came from as far as Mancheste

O'Connor as depicted on a banner

minutes for this procession to pass through the Kersal Bar as it turned into Moor Lane.

Manchester Guardian records say that over thirty bands took part in the various processions. The banners evoked many sentiments and included reference to the Peterloo Massacre, such as, 'The Sloughter of Our Unarmed and Peaceable Brethren on the Plains of Peterloo AD 1819.' The Leigh banner and the Oldham flag appealed to people to, 'Remember 18th August.1819, Peterloo,' and took six men to carry! The Bury contingent carried 13 flags, calling for 'Universal Suffrage,' 'Vote by Ballot' and declaring, 'Labour, The Source of all Wealth.' Some banners reminded people of the French Revolution with cries for 'Liberty and Fraternity' and were decorated with the French 'cap of liberty.'

Rochdale, Oldham, Stalybridge and Stockport, many walking. They were joined on the Moor by contingents from Bury, Bolton, Tottington, Unsworth and Middleton.

At 10.30am the Manchester procession started off, passing Strangeways and along the Bury New Road. It was led by a trumpeter on horse back, followed by a band and a banner declaring the five demands of the Charter. The various trade contingents, with their striking banners and more bands, were led by the Tailors, in one hundred and five files of five abreast, followed by the four hundred representatives of the Steam Engine Friendly Society.

Other groups included the Blacksmiths and the Wheelwrights and over eight hundred Dyers and Dressers from the textile trade, together with the Friendly Society of Cotton Spinners. The shoemakers, the most radical group, were there in force. It took 35

On arrival at the Moor, banners were propped up against the racecourse fencing and, to rousing cheers, the speeches commenced. Amongst the speakers were two from Salford: R.J. Richardson and R.B.Cobbett with John Fielden as the Chairman. The main Speaker was Feargus O'Connor. O'Connor called Parliament, 'a set of vagabond cowards!' and commented that, 'If the Whigs are devils, the Tories are devils in hell!'

Such speeches stirred the crowds and bonded the workers in solidarity. The confidence, which came from being part of a mass movement, gave those attending a sense of hope. As they left for home, about four o'clock, it started to rain, but the bands played on, maintaining a spirit of optimism and the feeling must have been that, 'things can only get better.' The New Song of the Great Demonstration, written in 1838, demonstrate the feelings and strength of the Chartist movement. It is a wonderful record of the day.[14]

A second rally on the Moor on 25th May 1839 saw fewer people, although at least 30,000 were recorded. There was a suspicion that numbers were swollen by those coming for the races to follow! Again rousing speeches were made by O'Connor and Dr. Taylor from Glasgow and the sense of moral righteousness was still strong. The discussion was mainly on the form the campaign should now take. The slogan, 'Peaceful if we can, forceful if we must!' was perhaps the problem. The difference was between those using moral and persuasive arguments [Owenites] and the militant section advocating more direct action. Whereas, at the first rally, there were only six police, who had been told not to interfere, for the second rally there were troops camped on the Moor, a sign that the authorities were getting anxious and ready to put down an 'worker revolt.'

Sadly, the fervour of the first rally was not maintained. In spite of a million signatures on a petition, it was rejected in Parliament. This was very demoralising for the leaders and led to more squabbling between them. The fact that there was a temporary revival in trade which reduced the number of unemployed, also influenced the working class support. Employers, although shaken by the display of worker strength, were still determined to resist any demands, which would interfere with their profits. Parliament firmly rejected the Charter, as being detrimental to its power and saw capitulation as a dangerous move.

KERSAL. BAR.

Kersal Bar in late 19th century.

In 1848 the National Petition [Charter] was presented to Parliament for the third time and was again rejected. This was devastating and very demoralising. The Government, fearful of reprisals, stationed the East Norfolk Regiment on the Moor from 1848, as part of a military presence in Lancashire and as a warning against future Chartist agitation.

In 1846 the Corn Laws and Navigation Acts had been repealed so that foreign ships could enter British ports. The dismantling of these trade barriers brought down the price of some goods and slightly helped to lessen tension.

However, the battle for suffrage and better conditions still continued for the rest of the century. The role of the Kersal Moor rallies was not insignificant. Engels recognised Kersal Moor as a, 'plebeian stronghold of the Manchester Chartists.' It was here that the five demands of the People's Charter had been endorsed and would be the driving force for political change for the next sixty years. [15 & 16]

THE NEXT HUNDRED YEARS ON THE MOOR

A Century of Building.

History doesn't stand still and the Moor saw many changes in the next hundred years. The land gradually descended to, or was bought by, the Clowes family, then Lords of the Manor of Broughton. From 1840 the Rev. John Clowes used his influence to increase his wealth by becoming the first developer of Broughton Park and Kersal. The Clowes family home was in Broughton Hall, with its private park, lake and zoo lying to the east of Bury New Road. He was active in building big houses for the new rich, high above the pollution and grime of Manchester, and drew in a vast income from rents from these properties. Many of these mansions were built on Clowes land on Vine Street or on Great Clowes Street in Broughton.

Interestingly, some of these same properties, which over recent years had fallen into dereliction, are now being redeveloped through the Salford Strategic Partnership, or by private developers and converted into apartments; a new era of wealth creation for a new group of entrepreneurs!

This current regeneration is a cause for social and political dispute over the policy of joint public and private financing, seen by some as disenfranchising the public. It is a debate again, between those who feel exploited and those out to maximise their profits. [17]

The Church returns to the Moor

The church influence returned with the building of St Paul's Church, in 1852. The idea of a church came from Colonel Clowes, the main landowner in the area, who thought his estate's employees should have somewhere to worship. He got permission from the Bishop of Manchester for the race-course grandstand to be used for worship on Sundays and to be a school in the week. He also paid the teachers' salaries and then set about raising funds for a church building.

To build a church was seen as a mark of status and also reinforced respect and gratitude, maintaining the hierarchy between employer and worker.

The local middle class subscribed to the fund and on 29th May 1852, the church was consecrated by the Bishop of Manchester and opened its doors to a

St Paul's Church, built 1852

full congregation of over 1,000 people. The land was donated by Colonel Clowes and Eleanora Atherton of Kersal Cell, as was the land for a school, to replace the temporary one still meeting in the Grandstand.

A school on the Moor

Initially a temporary building was put up, on the south side of Moor Lane then just a dirt track. The permanent building was built, on the opposite side of the lane, after a design competition won by the architect William Walker. I opened as an elementary school in 186 and did not close till 1974. It structure was church-like in appearance with small spires and gargoyles, as were many 'board' schools.

Board schools, built after the 1870 Education Act, established the first free and compulsory state education in England. So the St Paul's School was in advance of this development, as were many Church Schools in Victorian times. It also had two cottages presumably for a head teacher and caretaker.

St Paul's Church of England School 1871-1974, unknown photographer

Painting by Louis Susman (1978) of St Paul's old School now hanging in St Paul's new school

The Moor becomes Public Property

In 1888, Salford Council took over the management of the Moor, for public recreation, 'to be conserved in its rural state.' The Moor gradually changed.

The south side of Moor Lane was

Salford Football Ground.

given over to recreation and sport including tennis, archery and cricket. What is now the football pitch was a cricket ground and tennis was played on what is now the new St Paul's school playground. Rugby was later played on this site before it became the home of the Salford Football Club.

The north side of Moor Lane then became a place for leisurely walking and picnicking. A Pavilion or bandstand was built during this time and also a slate walled urinal just near the cemetery wall. Benches were placed on the highest points and water was piped to a drinking fountain, also near the church boundary. In fact, it was well set up for leisurely public use. Fencing, which was erected to stop the tipping of rubbish, provoked letters to *The Guardian* about whether it was necessary considering its high cost.

Kersal Moor water fountain

In 1897 the Moor was picked as the Manchester site for an enormous bonfire to celebrate the Diamond Jubilee of Queen Victoria and again in 1911 to commemorate the coronation of

Bonfire on Kersal Moor on the coronation of George V - From Salford Reporter, 24th June 1911

George V. This bonfire was fifty fee high and its base covered over 1,00 feet and could be seen for many mile around. The Moor was also the site fc another bonfire to celebrate th coronation of George VI in 1937.

The Moor starts to Shrink

From the 1840's the Clowes estat continued to be sold off, little by littl Vine Street, part of the Moor an Clowes estate, was the dividing bound ary between Kersal Moor and Kersa Dale, and was an increasingly popula road, because of the views it com manded. Here the wealthy uppe middle class built their large an imposing mansions, over-looking 'th Cliff' and the meadows down to th River Irwell. Nevile Road was then a unnamed dirt lane, referred to as 'bac of Vine Street.' It was, in fact, the bac door or tradesmen's entrance to man of these grand houses.

On this dirt lane Clowes built house for his employees. A mock Tudor row c terrace houses, called Prospect Row i still there today. Built in 1896, it backe onto the market gardens, which serve the Clowes house. The chief Gam Keeper lived in the tallest and centra house of the row and the rest house employees according to their impor tance. There are also employees' house at the bottom of Oaklands Road, whic still bear the coat-of-arms of the Clowe family.

Further along Nevile Road, is a ro of stables and coachman's house, no\ converted into cottages. These previ ously belonged to Heathbank, which i now a block of apartments called Nevil Court. Another block of apartments i on the site of Norwood, anothe impressive mansion. Further alon Vine Street is a very imposing mansior originally called 'the Hollies' and buil

Prospect Row

The Clowes Coat of Arms.

in 1861 by a William Chandler Bird, a merchant. In 1875 a Thomas Roberts, a drysalter, moved there and after his death his two daughters. They must have rattled around because it was truly enormous!

In 1913 it became Lancaster House and is now owned by the Government for legal services. To the rear and opening onto Nevile Road is the coach house and gardener's house, now private residences.

The rectory for the St Paul's Church, which had twenty-one rooms, was initially on this road, but it was later 'scaled-down' and rebuilt on Nevile Road and finally transferred to a modern property on Moorside Road, opposite the church. The old rectory was sold to the Church of England

Children Society, then called 'Waifs and Strays Society' being the Northern headquarters of the Society until 2004, when a modern block of apartments replaced it. The last habited grand house on Vine Street is 'Kersal Dale,' once called 'Thorncliffe,' and built in Italianate style in 1850. This became the HQ of the Manchester Automobile Association, followed by an 'all night' club called 'The Commercial.' Now it is a residential care home.

Kersal Dale Residential Home, once 'Thorncliffe.'

At the far end of Vine Street was Moorlands, another mansion, which was requisitioned for the Red Cross, during the 1st World War, to nurse injured soldiers. This later became a convent (sometimes referred to as a monastery) for a closed order of Carmelite nuns.

Cousins, the famous soap makers, also had their family home called Oaklands, just south of Vine Street. In 1920 Alexander Cousins transferred his factory of 'manufacturing chemists and drysalters' to Kersal, employing many local people. It is perhaps best known for its famous brand of soap, 'Imperial Leather,' which was created in 1917, as an order for the Russian Court, just before the Tsar and family were executed. This house was later demolished and Halls of Residence for Salford

University were built on the site in the late 1950's.

These big houses typified the wealth of the Manchester industrialists, bankers and merchants in the Victorian period.

Land was sold for development along Moor Lane and Nevile Road in the early 1900s, most of this building being carried out by Darlingtons, a local firm of reputable builders. The terrace houses in Nevile Road were built in 1911 and those backing them in Moor Lane, in the 1920's. Some of the more modern semis were built in the back gardens of the Vine Street mansions in the 1920's.[18]

A piece of land, adjacent to the church, was purchased in 1923 and given to the church, to prevent an electricity substation being built there. This little piece of 'forest' is 'the largest stand of beech trees in Salford.'[19]

The next building to the church is the previous Police Station, with its stables for the police horses at the back. This is now a private house. On the corner of Moor Lane and Bury New Road, is the little Toll House, converted to a general shop, after the tolls were removed. As a grade 2 listed building, it was renovated in 2006 and stands like a little white sentinel at the corner of Moor Lane. It's interesting that tolls,

The renovated toll house at Kersal bar

renamed 'congestion charges,' wer once again being considered along th road in 2008.

A small private nursery school, bui in Victorian times on the corner of Moc Lane and Nevile Road, still exists. It wa bought by the Spanish and Portugues Jewish community, as they moved ou of the Cheetham Hill area. It is now synagogue and community hall name the Lena and Werner Mayer Memori Hall, after the benefactors.

Finally, there is sad piece of 'hidde land, which was the Boardman Nursery. It is lost between the houses (Moor lane and Nevile Road and cannc be seen or easily accessed. It is a tang of weeds and bushes, and owned by th developer and millionaire Ale Langsam, who presumably is waitin for the 'right' time to bring it back int use.

A development of houses, just wher Moor Lane dips down to Rainsough an skirting the current Moor, on what i now Heathfield Road, was started jus before the 2nd World War and stoo without roofs for some years. Th completion of the buildings wa postponed till after the war and the extended over, what was known b children as, the 'little moor.'

All this development cut into th area of what was the 'ancient' Moor (over 100 acres. The Moor of today onl covers 12 acres and is enclosed by Moc Lane, Heathland Road, Singleto Brook and the Cemetery of the St Paul Church.

IN LIVING MEMORY

The present Moor, and the sur rounding area, which was once part c the Moor, has continued to chang during the lifetime of the curren population. Some of these changes hav

26

aused regret and dismay and some interesting controversy.

The stories that follow have not been written previously and are the memories and reminiscences of people alive today. Consequently, they reflect their opinions, their memories and experiences and may even have slight errors, because memory does not guarantee the truth.

The School on the Moor.

Let's start with the demolition of a building central to the history of the Moor, a building, which has played an important part in the lives of many local people. This was the St Paul's Church of England Primary School, built in 1861, closed in 1974 and demolished in the 980's.

Lack of investment in the school building led to its gradual deterioration. Some ex-pupils remember the leaking roof and the cold, cold classrooms, which did not have today's luxury of central heating. They remember the Head teacher having to run out to the telephone box, because there was no phone on site and they remember eating their dinners from their school desks. Others, however, have happy memories of small classes, lessons on the Moor on sunny days, nature walks, sports days on the Football Ground and even watching Father Christmas trudge his way across the snowy Moor, with his sack of gifts. One person remembered extra-curricula visits to the Isle of Man and even far-away Dorset! The school population, a little over 100 children, was a mixed one, not selected from Church of England followers.

Catholics and little children from the local Jewish population were happily welcomed, even though the Vicar from St Paul's called in each week

and Church meetings were regularly held on the school premises.

Ex-pupils remember their teachers, especially Miss Holsworth, the last head teacher. The ethos seemed to be one of belonging, being friendly and, because it was small, feeling secure.

The land the school was built on had been given to the church by Colonel Clowes and Miss Atherton of Kersal Cell, in 1851. When the school came up for sale Salford Council declined to buy it, because of the expensive repairs needed and because it wasn't big enough for the growing child population of the area. Also the Council already owned land opposite with access from Nevile Road. For a time the old school reopened as a private nursery, with the two schoolhouses still being rented.

Eventually it was put up for sale by the Bishop of Manchester and the trustees of the Clowes Estate and bought by the local property developer, Alex Langsam.

The new school was built next to the football ground on what was then used by the Langworthy Rugby League Club. This was built to a very different style from its predecessor and was opened in 1976, by the then Prime Minister, James Callaghan.

New St Paul's School, Nevile Road

A New Road & a Fight for Trees

It was the building of this new school that led to the surface improvements of Nevile Road. Whereas the road was tarmac up to the school from the Moor Lane end and the kerbs were laid the full length, the residents at the other end of Nevile Road had to pay for the road to be adopted and surfaced. This was in 1977 and, although the residents saw the advantages, they felt aggrieved at the £70 they had to pay for something, which they saw as a very public amenity.

These road improvements meant cutting into the football ground and building an embankment to take the pavement, which now runs along the side of the field. Trees then became the focus of a dispute. The Kersal residents were angry at the thought of losing the Manchester poplar trees, which had grown just within the sports field and were cut down to make way for the footpath. There was quite an outcry and the Kersal Residents Association demanded compensation.

The Salford 'arboriculturalist' happened to live in the area and was, therefore, quite vulnerable to the agitation from the Association. He was 'persuaded' to rectify this loss. Some 'Swedish White Beams,' which are quite rare and expensive trees, had been purchased by Manchester Council for the pedestrianisation of Kings Street. Salford Council bought these, at great expense! They now line the embankment in all their glory.

You just can't cut down trees without a public outcry!

The number 154 bus, from Bury to the North Manchester Hospital, now runs along the road and this, plus the congestion of parked cars, especially on football nights, may make many residents wish it was still an unmade country lane!

Back to the School

We have not yet finished with the story of the St Paul's School! The saga continues!

There had been an on-going concern over planning permission for building on the school site. In 1993 the Moor was granted the status of being 'a site of biological importance' (SBI) and Salford also recorded its intentions to preserve it as a local Nature Reserve. However, the school site, which was privately owned, was not covered by this ruling.

The site now lies as a patch of dangerous rubble and brick debris. It was never fully cleared after its demolition, presumably because the owner intended building there. Colonising plants such as rosebay willow herb, ivy and even shrubs do soften the appearance, but that does not really hide the shambles left by the demolition. Any thought of new development on the site brings out a cry of resistance from those who respect the history of the Moor and value its natural beauty.

As early as 1972 there had been a dispute over the status of the Moor and whether it could be registered as 'common land,' under the Common Registration Act 1965. A Mr Yeomans of Lower Broughton and the Parent Teachers Association of St Paul's School on the Moor had registered the Cliff and Kersal Moor as common land, being land on which the inhabitants' had 'indulged in sports and pastimes as of right for not less than 20 years.' This was disputed, at Council meetings because it meant that the Council would lose all rights for any future development. The Council challenged it on the

28

ounds that it was not a 'village green.' he school PTA took up the fight under ιe Chairmanship of the Rev, Dudley lades of Weaste. The conclusion to this ispute has been lost in bureaucracy!

This vagueness added to the public oncern about the possibility of future uilding on the Moor

Dr William Kitchingman, who has ved in Kersal all his life, recorded this ublic anxiety. In a letter, written on 3th March 1980, to the Salford City ouncil Planning Department, he xpressed his strong feelings about the ossible demolition of the building and ιe planning application for 12 houses) be built on the site.

A petition, organised by Dr ιitchingman, containing over 200 ignatures, was presented to the ouncil by Councillor Rufus Heron and ιpported by County Councillor Jack lenry. Dr Kitchingman, personally, ad no objection to the school itself eing renovated and used, but felt that ιe building of new houses might start a rend' for further building and the eath toll of the Moor.

The anger of the petitioners was ιcorded in 23rd May's Salford City .eporter, under the heading, 'Resi-ents urge: don't spoilt the country-ide.' This article referred to the ossibility of houses being built on the ite by Everbuild Ltd., for the owner .lex Langsam.

Dr Kitchingman tried a parallel ιctic. On 14th May 1980, he wrote to ιe Department of the Environment, equesting that the building be consid-red for listing, as being of architectural nd historical interest.

Sadly, the building was not ιccepted, possibly because it had been ιandalised badly whilst empty and parts of the building looted.

Demolition started in early 1980s, before the actual planning permission had been fully granted! As one of the oldest schools in Salford and one with close ties to the St. Paul's Church, it was regrettable that funds could not be found for its renovation, even if it had been put to a different use.

The petition was partially successful however, because the number of houses was reduced to five from the twelve previously granted and the new permission stated that the cottages should be renovated and incorporated in the development. That was the situation in March 1981.

Now in 2008, the land is still an unsightly patch of rubble. The Friends of Kersal Moor wrote to Mr Langsam to find out his intentions with no success. Over 20 years after he had made the original application for planning the land remains untouched.

To clarify the present situation, a letter was sent to the Salford Chief Planning Officer in August 2008, asking for an update on the situation. The reply stated that, 'as no further application has been received since the original and, as it is now allocated within the Unitary Development Plan [EN8/9] Nature Conservation Sites of Local Importance, it would be difficult now to secure planning permission.' The reply also stated that the original permission was granted for 28 houses, but no reference was made to the two cottages, which were apparently illegally pulled down.

One hopes this will be a satisfactory end to the story, which has occupied many people for over twenty-five years. Now all that remains is the clearing of the site.

The New School fights for its life

The 'new' St Paul's primary school, on Nevile Road, was also under threat in early 2003 when it was leaked that it may be amalgamated with the Lower Kersal School and the site made into a carpark! Parents were very angry because they had not been consulted and, together with the church, led a powerful drive to reverse this policy. They were successful! It seems you can't tangle with the Kersal residents without a fight.

Goodbye to the Nuns

Another building, which has disappeared in the last twenty-five years, is Moorlands, the Carmelite Convent, which was accessed via Vine Street and backed onto Nevile Road. This became a Convent in April 1920 and was demolished in March 1993. People have fascinating tales to tell of this closed, silent community of Carmelite nuns.

Some children were a little scared, because of its 'strangeness.' Paul Cheadle, who now lives in Prospect Row, remembers, 'running up nunnery hill, peeping over the wall and running off if a nun came out!' Trevor Tomlinson, however, who lived at the rear of the Convent, developed a friendship with Sister Veronica and Sister Marie Theresa, the two nuns allowed to speak to the public. As a young boy he ran regular errands and did little jobs for them.

Another Nevile Road resident, remembers going to the Convent with children, to deliver harvest festival food and Sister Veronica opening her little 'hatch' window to thank them. She remembers seeing the young nuns over the wall, lining up as they collected the laundry from the line. She reflecte 'They were a very self-sufficier community' and she was, 'sad to see th Convent closed.' She and other loc residents visited the Convent during th demolition and observed the severity the nun's existence.

Trevor, as an adult, persuaded th demolition workers to let him into th grounds so he was able to record the la days of the building. I'm sure he fe some sadness as he relived his visits u the big steps to the heavy front door. H pictures show an impressive, althoug stark interior and grounds that wei quite beautiful with flowering shrul and fruit trees.

Front door to the convent,
prior to demolition

Joe and Maureen Tobin, froi Number 2 Nevile Road, which was the a corner shop, also had a relationshi with the nuns, since they delivered th weekly bread order. They remembere Sister Veronica as 'a little round lad with her little dog, which was reall irritable and yapped at everyone!' an according to Sister Veronica, 'it shoulc n't be a convent dog!' Doris Boustead who also lives on Nevile Road and wa the last owner of the fish and chip sho at the bottom of Oaklands Road, tells c the weekly visit of Sister Veronica t collect fish and chips for the nun:

emolition of the convent, showing ld brick wall on Nevile Road

However, she doesn't remember any ayment!

In 1992 the Convent was closed. As iere had been many alterations to the uilding it could not be listed. There ere no 'mod cons' in the Convent and so the few remaining nuns, who irvived a frugal existence, were then derly.

The demolition of the Convent egan with less of a public outcry than or the school. However, some con- erned residents of Nevile Road, who, hen they heard that the builders itended removing the wall which irrounded the Convent, certainly ade a fuss. So now this beautiful

ateway used to deliver nuns food

historic wall remains. Opposite 36 Nevile Road you will see the little arched door-way, now bricked-up, which was an access point for the delivery of food for the nuns.

The site now has 30 modern houses on two cul-de-sacs named Tuscany View and Degas Close. Much as I like Tuscany and admire Degas, it seems a pity that more relevant names could not have been chosen; names that reflect the history of the area.

Things that go 'bump in the night'

There is an interesting and, to some, an eerie story left to tell. Close to these houses and part of the development, is a walled garden, with a small arched doorway and locked gate. Inside it is dark and overgrown because the trees have been left undisturbed. They search for the light and their branches over- flow the walls that once surrounded the convent.

Entrance to the 'secret garden'

Although each resident has a key to this 'secret garden' few use it. Is this because the builders unearthed bones there? Although the bones turned out to be animal bones and a church service with prayers was held, it has not removed the doubts of some people, who believe this little 'secret garden' could be haunted! Anthony and Loretta

Litle, who live in the first house, next to this plot, are happy to be its neighbour, since it guarantees quiet and privacy and interesting bird life. Some other residents however, speak of strange 'cold' sensations!

Another Tree Story

Above the high wall surrounding the Convent site on Nevile Road, tower 16 'Manchester' poplar trees.' These magnificent specimens are what is known nationally as the 'black poplar,' and are some of a dwindling number in the Manchester area. These trees were widely planted in the 19th century and believed to have been planted originally by Neolithic settlers from a stock of two or three trees.

Poplar trees from Nevile Road

This very narrow genetic base mak them vulnerable to disease. Howeve because they were particularly resista to the effects of pollution they becam popular tree for planting in par during Victorian times. In 2000, the were about 7,000 around Manchest and Salford. In that year a virule strain of poplar fungus, was notic attacking the trees. It was feared th this tree population would be extin within ten years. Such a catastrop would have changed the landscape Manchester and Salford. In 200 conservation staff from Kew Garden based at Wakefield Place, ne Ardingly, donated 7,000 mature fema trees to the Red Rose Communi Forest in Manchester to safeguard tl future of the trees. It is now an impo tant Kew Gardens conservation proje and is being carefully monitored.

The people on Nevile Road love tl trees for their grace and changir foliage, but the residents of Tuscar View, say that they interfere with the TV reception. Two trees have bee removed, but now a watchful eye being kept on the others. Although isn't something people argue about, tl ecological value of the trees, pl 'climate change' and its possib repercussions, mean that these ve special trees have a strong case.[20] .

Fire and Disaster

1970 and 80's saw dramatic chang to St Paul's Church. In the early 1970 Salford Council decided to clean a public buildings, removing the crin and smoke dirt of a century. Tl church's newly revealed light stor stood out against the green of the Moo creating an impressive picture. The disaster struck! Twice it was vandalise by arson attacks; once in 1982, whic gutted part of the interior and, tl cond time, in 1987, fortunately when e church was empty. This was more rious and destroyed part of the roof, e stained glass windows and melted e organ pipes. The bell, which eighed nearly a ton, crashed through e tower, shattering the stone font and nbedding itself into the floor. The wer and the spire were so dangerously eak that, for four years, services were ld in the new school. As the church is grade 2 listed building great care was ken to preserve its architecture. A assive steel collar was used to ensure e tower remained safe, during its pair. The interior was remodelled to a ore modern design and is now open an with space and light.

The vandals responsible for the fire ere never found and now the church is cked, whereas previously it was open all times. [21]

Rest in Peace

Whilst we think about the church it worth taking a walk around the metery. This brings many surprises. seems that, even in death, people like e thought of being 'laid to rest' where e air is fresh and unpolluted. The metery has been extended twice and me of the oldest gravestones are now st in thick vegetation. I was informed at graves of soldiers, who died in the o world wars, are entitled to £13 each r their maintenance. This fund viously helps with the on-going aintenance of this large cemetery of er 4,000 graves.

Amongst the many famous people ried there is Edwin Waugh, the alect expert, who specifically quested this burial site, since it minded him of his Rossendale home. he Guardian reported that 20,000 ople lined the Bury New Road for his neral procession from Victoria

St. Paul's Church during repairs

Station. Also there, are the graves of William Axon, the founder of the Vegetarian Society, Dr Thomas Radford, who pioneered the use of Caesarian Section in childbirth and the Cusson's family. Other graves include Dr Robert Angus Smith, the first person to record 'acid rain' and also Henry Edward Schunk, a scientist, whose laboratory in his home in Vine Street, is now part of Manchester University. It is so popular, as a burial ground, that there are four Lord Mayors and even a Salford MP!

The most intriguing burial is that of a horse! Equine remains with bit and bridle were unearthed in 1936 but there is no record to tell us the story. One assumes that, when a horse died or was badly injured, they would be shot and buried 'on the spot.'

The fact that the iron railings around

33

the church and the cemetery were not removed, for munitions during the war, is a sign that someone had influence in high places!

Goodbye to 'The Kersal'.

A building, which served as a sort of community centre for over 200 years, was the Turf Tavern, built originally on farmland and owned by the Clowes estate. It had brewed its own beer at the rear of the buildings, where later two prime bowling greens were developed. It was renamed in 1893, as the Kersal Moor Hotel, when bought at auction, by Boddingtons. This soon became 'The Kersal.' It stood on this site until it was demolished in 2003, making way for a modern block of 37 apartments called Lever Court. Some elderly residents regret its demise, missing it as a familiar place 'for a chat and a pint.' Others feel it had deteriorated and become noisy and rough. Whatever the opinion, it was an elegant building which had witnessed many historic events, some exciting and some macabre.

The Kersal Hotel, now demolished

The Famous and the Notorious

The Moor has had some media fame in living memory. Gert and Daisy [Elsie and Doris Walters of radio fame] attended the opening of the Heathfield Road houses in 1938. [22]

In 1962 the film, ' A Kind of Loving,' featuring Alan Bates, was partial filmed at 2 Heathfield Road, the hor of Mr and Mrs Rosenbloom. Mo recently, in 2005, Robson Green join the players from Salford Football Tea in the filming of the series, 'Northe Lights' and some shots in 'Shameles the popular TV series, were filmed (Oakland's Road. Also Ray Winstone h been seen in the area.

And then, of course, Salford Ci Football Club is always in the news a searching for fame!

Now for the notorious!

In the 1970s there was a politic scandal involving the leader of t Liberal party, Jeremy Thorpe and h supposed 'lover' Norman Scott. Sc accused Thorpe of a plan to murd him, because he threatened to disclo their friendship. [This friendship ha occurred in the early 1960's, when su relationships were illegal.] Actually h Great Dane dog was shot rather tha any person, but it was a story of extrem media interest, since it involved oth government ministers. Where does t Moor come into this unsavoury stor Well Blackfields Lane between Nev Road and Vine Street was rumoured be Norman Scott's hideout from t media! This very old, little dark alley a road was a perfect hideout. W would think of looking there?

CHILDREN'S MEMORIE

Finally, it is time for us to see t Moor through the eyes of the childre who have romped across its 'ups a downs,' over the centuries. Charl Roeder, in his record of 1907, talked o flocks of merry children, romping a burrowing and rolling in the sandy a grassy flanks.' Present day adults al have happy memories of doing 'doub roly-polies' down the sand hills,

imbing the trees and den building
ider some of the bushy spots that
lults couldn't get to! They all talk of
aying on the 'the beach' and even
king their buckets and spades there.
ne elderly resident of Moor Lane
miniscd, telling me of the very
atural way' he wet the sand for his
sters to make better sand pies! In fact,
is remembered by many as an area
at was 'nearly all sand when we were
ds.' 'With its fresh, bracing air, it was,
ke going to Blackpool!'

andy 'beach' on the Moor

The last owners of the Nevile Road
op remembered children popping in
r liquorice root and lemonade, on
eir way to the Moor. There children
ould spend hours with their friends
aying chasing and hide and seek,
siting 'Blackie Brook,' and 'just
essing about.' This brook, so named
y the children after the Myrtle Grove
ye Works, owned by Blackies, is
tually Singleton Brook. It acts as the
oundary between Salford and Bury
ouncils. It was often a 'stream of many
olours' when the dyes were released,
lding to its fascination. One resident
membered it as 'awful and smelly!

However, two large purpose-built
servoirs, also belonging to Blackies,
tracted swans and ducks and were
ell known for good swimming and
fishing. These have been filled in now
and the area is an industrial site behind
the Carphone Warehouse. Other
reservoirs, which were near to the path
going up to the Heathlands Residential
Home, from the northwest corner of the
Moor, were also filled in. If one goes
that way one needs 'wellies' as it is
always like a swamp.

A young man, who grew up in
Kersal, Christopher Carroll, whilst
finalising his plans for emigrating to
Australia, reflected happily about
playing on the Moor with his pals. He
was leaving with very happy memories
of his childhood on Kersal Moor, unlike
James Billington who, nearly 200 years
previously, was transported, as a
punishment and against his will, to the
very same continent. How things
change!

Bugsy, Rabbits and Foxes.

Memories from childhood include
'hunting for rabbits' because there are
many on the Moor, hiding under the
thick gorse and burrowing in the soft
sandy soil. Especially mentioned is
'Bugsy', the black and white, once pet
rabbit, which would come out and
watch people. Sadly it is no longer seen.

If you are lucky you may spot a fox,
prowling for its supper in the early
hours of the evening and at night you
will hear owls and notice many bats.

Conkers and Rubbish

The pathway, running parallel to the
stream and ending at steps to Bury New
Road, seems only to be frequented by
children, in the autumn, for conker
collecting from the huge horse chestnut
trees, which keep this pathway dark and
damp. It is often used as a short cut, to
and fro, between Bury New Road and
the houses on the further edge of the
Moor. Sadly, it has become a spot for

litter, drink cans and other 'take-away' junk from the cafes and shops of Sedgley Park. Both its darkness and the litter act as a deterrent to walkers and it is one of the problems being tackled by the Friends of Kersal Moor.

Sadly, a change has come over the Moor as a children's playground. Now it's mostly frequented by adults walking their dogs. Recently teenagers tried to make the Moor a track for their 'off-road motorised bikes,' which churned up the pathways and polluted the quiet. In 2007 notices went up warning of immediate confiscation. So now they find the Moor 'boring.'

A different life-style has developed for younger children over the last 20 years. They no longer play with the same freedom, as did their parents and grand parents. They are more closely protected and parents tend to see the quiet and the shady places of the Moor as potentially dangerous. The children ride their bikes near their homes, play in their gardens or watch television.

Old style games with freedom and imagination have gone. In its place are the organised children's activities provided by the Salford Park Rangers, such as the annual Teddy Bears Picnic and kite making and flying. Usually children come to these activities with their parents and rarely are childr[en] seen playing by themselves. It is a ve[ry] sad fact the Moor is no longer a place [of] fun and freedom.

There are no buildings on the Mo[or] now; the Pavilion was vandalised, bur[nt] down and finally removed. All but o[ne] of the old benches remains and t[he] men's toilet and the drinking founta[in] have disappeared. So the Moor h[as] returned to its rural origins, unclu[t]tered by any such amenities. The on[ly] facilities are special bins for dog litter [at] each entrance to the Moor.

The responsibility for the Coun[cil] has become one of maintenance and [?] preservation as a natural habitat. [In] 1997/8 the Salford 'Ground Wor[k]' team, did some maintenance on t[he] pathways, digging in timber to act [as] steps and netting areas to conserve t[he] slopes, which were slowly being erode[d]. Since that time the Friends of Kers[al] Moor, reformed in 2006, have taken [on] some of the responsibility for th[e] preservation, with regular litter clear[,] path maintenance, some tree manag[e]ment and a plan for restoring seat[s.] Campaigning for better supervision [to] stop tipping at the Bury New Roa[d] entrance and along Church Lan[e] between the old Police station and t[he] Church, is also one of its aims.

The Friends built one rustic ty[pe] bench in 2007, with materials from t[he] Council and their volunteer labour. Th[is] was carefully situated so that the spi[re] of the church can be seen but the sig[ht] smell and noise of the Moor Lane traf[fic] cannot. There are plans for more seat[s] which will be appreciated by some of t[he] elderly people, who walk the Moor.

The Friends also hold informati[on] sessions on the flora and fauna and t[he] history of the Moor and there are ide[as] to commemorate its rich history wi[th]

Teddy Bear's Picnic on the Moor.

nch built by Friends of Kersal
oor in 2008.

e possible positioning of a Blue
aque and special Notice Boards.

If there is a fraction of the enthusi-
m of the big political rallies of the 19th
ntury then this could all happen.

In May 2009 the Friends of Kersal

Moor hosted a celebration event on the
moor.

As we come to the end of our little
tour across time and dwell on the
colourful history of the Moor, we can
claim, without any doubt, that it is
worthy of recognition for the part it has
played in the history of Salford and
Manchester and, perhaps, even the
nation.

May it continue to be a place to walk,
to dream and relax away from the stress
and the noise that surrounds it. May
the people of Kersal remember its
history and forever protect this unique
patch of land.

As Charles Roeder said, 'There is no
other spot bound up with so much
romance.'

rsal Moor under snow. winter 2008

THE BIO-DIVERSITY OF KERSAL MOO

The Greater Manchester Ecology Unit described Kersal Moor as a 'mosaic of acid grassland and lowland heath with small areas of neutral grasslan which has retained a natural character in an inner city area. Acid grassland and lowland heath are UK Biodiversity Priority Habitats.' The following is a list of th plants and trees recorded on the Moor by the Unit in 2006 fo Salford City Counc

Norway Maple	**Cocksfoot**	**Moss**
Acer platanoides	*Dactylis glomerata*	*Polyrichum juniperinum*
Sycamore	**Wavy hair grass**	**Moss**
Acer pseudoplatanus	*Deschampsia flexuosa*	*Polytrichum piliferum*
Common bent	**Crowberry**	**Cherry**
Agrostis capillaries	*Empetrum nigrum*	*Prunus x avium*
Creeping bent	**Beech**	**Oak**
Agrostis stolonifera	*Fagus sylvatica*	*Quercus robur*
Common alder	**Sheeps fescue**	**Creeping buttercup**
Alnus glutinosa	*Festuca ovina*	*Ranunculus repens*
False oat	**Forsythia**	**Rhododendron**
Arrhenathrum elatius	*Forsythia x intermedia*	*Rhododendron ponticum*
Mugwort	**Ash**	**Japanese rose**
Artemisia vulgaris	*Fraxinus excelsior*	*Rosa rugosa*
Michaelmas daisy	**Manna ash**	**Bramble**
Aster novi-belgii	*Fraxinus ornus*	*Rubus fruticosus*
Spotted laurel	**Yorkshire fog**	**Sheeps sorrel**
Aucuba japonica	*Holcus lanatus*	*Rumex acetosella*
Silver birch	**Cats ear**	**Broad leaved dock**
Betula verrucosa	*Hypocharis radicata*	*Rumex obtusifolius*
Heather	**Holly**	**Goat willow**
Calluna vulgaris	*Ilex aquifolium*	*Salix caprea*
Moss	**Soft rush**	**Elder**
Campylopus introflexus	*Juncus effuses*	*Sambucus nigra*
Common sedge	**Heath rush**	**Stonecrop**
Carex nigra	*Juncus squarrosus*	*Sedum anglicum*
Hornbeam	**Laburnum**	**Ragwort**
Carpinus betulus	*Laburnum x anagyroides*	*Senecio jacobaea*
Sweet chestnut	**Garden privet**	**Whitebeam**
Castanea sativa	*Ligustrum ovalifolium*	*Sorbus aria*
Common centaury	**Greater birds foot trefoil**	**Rowan**
Centaurium erythraea	*Lotus pedunculatus*	*Sorbus aucuparia*
Rosebay willow herb	**Purple moor grass**	**Lilac**
Chamerion angustifolium	*Molinia caerula*	*Syringa x vulgaris*
Creeping thistle	**Mat grass**	**Dandilion**
Cirsium arvense	*Nardus stricta*	*Taraxacum officinale*
Lichens	**Ribwort**	**Red clover**
Cladonia spp	*lantago lanceolata*	*Trifolium pratense*
Hazel	**Bistort**	**White clover**
Corylus avellana	*Polygonum bistora*	*Trifolium repens*
Broom	**Moss**	**Gorse**
Cytisus scoparius	*Polytrichum commune*	*Ulex europaeus*